Daily
Time Sheet
Log Book

Belongs to

Name:

Adress:

Business Adress:

Email:

Mobile Telephone:

Home Telephone:

Fax:

Time sheet log book

Name: _____	Month/Time :

Day	Date		Time In	Time Out	Total Hours

Time sheet log book

Name: _____	Month/Time :

Day	Date		Time In	Time Out	Total Hours

Time sheet log book

Name: _____	Month/Time :

Day	Date		Time In	Time Out	Total Hours

Time sheet log book

Name: ____	Month/Time :

Day	Date		Time In	Time Out	Total Hours

Time sheet log book

Name: _____			Month/Time :		
Day	Date		Time In	Time Out	Total Hours

Time sheet log book

Name: _____	Month/Time :

Day	Date		Time In	Time Out	Total Hours

Time sheet log book

Name: _____	Month/Time :

Day	Date		Time In	Time Out	Total Hours

Time sheet log book

Name: _____

Month/Time :

Day	Date		Time In	Time Out	Total Hours

Time sheet log book

Name: _____			Month/Time :		
Day	**Date**		**Time In**	**Time Out**	**Total Hours**

Time sheet log book

Name: _____

Month/Time :

Day	Date		Time In	Time Out	Total Hours

Time sheet log book

Name: _____	Month/Time :

Day	Date		Time In	Time Out	Total Hours

Time sheet log book

Name: _____ Month/Time :

Day	Date		Time In	Time Out	Total Hours

Time sheet log book

Name: _____	Month/Time :

Day	Date		Time In	Time Out	Total Hours

Time sheet log book

Name: _____			Month/Time :		
Day	Date		Time In	Time Out	Total Hours

Time sheet log book

Name: _____	Month/Time :

Day	Date		Time In	Time Out	Total Hours

Time sheet log book

Name: ____	Month/Time :

Day	Date		Time In	Time Out	Total Hours

Time sheet log book

Name: _____ Month/Time :

Day	Date		Time In	Time Out	Total Hours

Time sheet log book

Name: _____			Month/Time :		
Day	**Date**		**Time In**	**Time Out**	**Total Hours**

Time sheet log book

Name: _____	Month/Time :

Day	Date		Time In	Time Out	Total Hours

Time sheet log book

Name: ____	Month/Time :

Day	Date		Time In	Time Out	Total Hours

Time sheet log book

Name: _____	Month/Time :

Day	Date		Time In	Time Out	Total Hours

Time sheet log book

Name: _____			Month/Time :		
Day	**Date**		**Time In**	**Time Out**	**Total Hours**

Time sheet log book

Name: _____	Month/Time :

Day	Date		Time In	Time Out	Total Hours

Time sheet log book

Name: _____			Month/Time :		
Day	**Date**		**Time In**	**Time Out**	**Total Hours**

Time sheet log book

Name: _____ | Month/Time :

Day	Date		Time In	Time Out	Total Hours

Time sheet log book

Name: ____ Month/Time :

Day	Date		Time In	Time Out	Total Hours

Time sheet log book

Name: _____			Month/Time :		
Day	**Date**		**Time In**	**Time Out**	**Total Hours**

Time sheet log book

Name: ____	Month/Time :

Day	Date		Time In	Time Out	Total Hours

Time sheet log book

Name: ____			Month/Time :		
Day	**Date**		**Time In**	**Time Out**	**Total Hours**

Time sheet log book

Name: _____ | Month/Time :

Day	Date		Time In	Time Out	Total Hours

Time sheet log book

Name: _____			Month/Time :		
Day	**Date**		**Time In**	**Time Out**	**Total Hours**

Time sheet log book

Name: _____			Month/Time :		
Day	**Date**		**Time In**	**Time Out**	**Total Hours**

Time sheet log book

Name: _____			Month/Time :		
Day	**Date**		**Time In**	**Time Out**	**Total Hours**

Time sheet log book

Name: _____			Month/Time :		
Day	**Date**		**Time In**	**Time Out**	**Total Hours**

Time sheet log book

Name: _____			Month/Time :		
Day	**Date**		**Time In**	**Time Out**	**Total Hours**

Time sheet log book

Name: _____	Month/Time :

Day	Date		Time In	Time Out	Total Hours

Time sheet log book

Name: _____ | Month/Time :

Day	Date		Time In	Time Out	Total Hours

Time sheet log book

Name: _____			Month/Time :		
Day	**Date**		**Time In**	**Time Out**	**Total Hours**

Time sheet log book

Name: _____	Month/Time :

Day	Date		Time In	Time Out	Total Hours

Time sheet log book

Name: _____	Month/Time :

Day	Date		Time In	Time Out	Total Hours

Time sheet log book

Name: _____

Month/Time :

Day	Date		Time In	Time Out	Total Hours

Time sheet log book

Name: _____ | Month/Time :

Day	Date		Time In	Time Out	Total Hours

Time sheet log book

Name: _____	Month/Time :

Day	Date		Time In	Time Out	Total Hours

Time sheet log book

Name: _____	Month/Time :

Day	Date		Time In	Time Out	Total Hours

Time sheet log book

Name: _____	Month/Time :

Day	Date		Time In	Time Out	Total Hours

Time sheet log book

Name: _____ | Month/Time :

Day	Date		Time In	Time Out	Total Hours

Time sheet log book

Name: _____ | Month/Time :

Day	Date		Time In	Time Out	Total Hours

Time sheet log book

Name: _____ **Month/Time :**

Day	Date		Time In	Time Out	Total Hours

Time sheet log book

Name: _____	Month/Time :

Day	Date		Time In	Time Out	Total Hours

Time sheet log book

Name: ____			Month/Time :		
Day	**Date**		**Time In**	**Time Out**	**Total Hours**

Time sheet log book

Name: _____			Month/Time :		
Day	**Date**		**Time In**	**Time Out**	**Total Hours**

Time sheet log book

Name: ____ | Month/Time :

Day	Date		Time In	Time Out	Total Hours

Time sheet log book

Name: _____	Month/Time :

Day	Date		Time In	Time Out	Total Hours

Time sheet log book

Name: ____ Month/Time :

Day	Date		Time In	Time Out	Total Hours

Time sheet log book

Name: _____			Month/Time :		
Day	Date		Time In	Time Out	Total Hours

Time sheet log book

Name: _____			Month/Time :		
Day	Date		Time In	Time Out	Total Hours

Time sheet log book

Name: _____	Month/Time :

Day	Date		Time In	Time Out	Total Hours

Time sheet log book

Name: _____			Month/Time :		
Day	**Date**		**Time In**	**Time Out**	**Total Hours**

Time sheet log book

Name: _____	Month/Time :

Day	Date		Time In	Time Out	Total Hours

Time sheet log book

Name: ____ | **Month/Time :**

Day	Date		Time In	Time Out	Total Hours

Time sheet log book

Name: _____	Month/Time :

Day	Date		Time In	Time Out	Total Hours

Time sheet log book

Name: _____ | Month/Time :

Day	Date		Time In	Time Out	Total Hours

Time sheet log book

Name: _____	Month/Time :

Day	Date		Time In	Time Out	Total Hours

Time sheet log book

Name: _____			Month/Time :		
Day	Date		Time In	Time Out	Total Hours

Time sheet log book

Name: _____ Month/Time :

Day	Date		Time In	Time Out	Total Hours

Time sheet log book

Name: _____			Month/Time :		
Day	Date		Time In	Time Out	Total Hours

Time sheet log book

Name: _____			Month/Time :		
Day	Date		Time In	Time Out	Total Hours

Time sheet log book

Name: _____			Month/Time :		
Day	**Date**		**Time In**	**Time Out**	**Total Hours**

Time sheet log book

Name: _____	Month/Time :

Day	Date		Time In	Time Out	Total Hours

Time sheet log book

Name: _____	Month/Time :

Day	Date		Time In	Time Out	Total Hours

Time sheet log book

Name: _____	Month/Time :

Day	Date		Time In	Time Out	Total Hours

Time sheet log book

Name: _____			Month/Time :		
Day	**Date**		**Time In**	**Time Out**	**Total Hours**

Time sheet log book

Name: _____	Month/Time :

Day	Date		Time In	Time Out	Total Hours

Time sheet log book

Name: _____ | Month/Time :

Day	Date		Time In	Time Out	Total Hours

Time sheet log book

Name: _____

Month/Time :

Day	Date		Time In	Time Out	Total Hours

Time sheet log book

Name: _____			Month/Time :		
Day	**Date**		**Time In**	**Time Out**	**Total Hours**

Time sheet log book

Name: _____	Month/Time :

Day	Date		Time In	Time Out	Total Hours

Time sheet log book

Name: _____			Month/Time :		
Day	Date		Time In	Time Out	Total Hours

Time sheet log book

Name: _____			Month/Time :		
Day	**Date**		**Time In**	**Time Out**	**Total Hours**

Time sheet log book

Name: _____			Month/Time :		
Day	Date		Time In	Time Out	Total Hours

Time sheet log book

Name: _____	Month/Time :

Day	Date		Time In	Time Out	Total Hours

Time sheet log book

Name: _____			Month/Time :		
Day	**Date**		**Time In**	**Time Out**	**Total Hours**

Time sheet log book

Name: _____	Month/Time :

Day	Date		Time In	Time Out	Total Hours

Time sheet log book

Name: _____ Month/Time :

Day	Date		Time In	Time Out	Total Hours

Time sheet log book

Name: _____			Month/Time :		
Day	**Date**		**Time In**	**Time Out**	**Total Hours**

Time sheet log book

Name: ____	Month/Time :

Day	Date		Time In	Time Out	Total Hours

Time sheet log book

Name: _____	Month/Time :

Day	Date		Time In	Time Out	Total Hours

Time sheet log book

Name: ____			Month/Time :		
Day	**Date**		**Time In**	**Time Out**	**Total Hours**

Time sheet log book

Name: _____			Month/Time :		
Day	**Date**		**Time In**	**Time Out**	**Total Hours**

Time sheet log book

Name: _____	Month/Time :

Day	Date		Time In	Time Out	Total Hours

Time sheet log book

Name: _____	Month/Time :

Day	Date		Time In	Time Out	Total Hours

Time sheet log book

Name: _____			Month/Time :		
Day	**Date**		**Time In**	**Time Out**	**Total Hours**

Time sheet log book

Name: _____	Month/Time :

Day	Date		Time In	Time Out	Total Hours

Time sheet log book

Name: _____			Month/Time :		
Day	Date		Time In	Time Out	Total Hours

Thank you!

WE ARE GLAD THAT YOU PURCHASED OUR BOOK!
PLEASE LET US KNOW HOW WE CAN IMPROVE IT!
YOUR FEEDBACK IS ESSENTIAL TO US.

Contact us at:

log'Sin@gmail.com

JUST TITLE THE EMAIL 'CREATIVE' AND WE WILL GIVE YOU SOME EXTRA SURPRISES!

www.ingramcontent.com/pod-product-compliance
Lightning Source LLC
Chambersburg PA
CBHW051759200326
41597CB00025B/4623
* 9 7 8 1 8 0 3 8 5 2 5 4 6 *